S0-AUJ-771

The Nonprofit Chief Executive's

TEN BASIC RESPONSIBILITIES

By **Rick Moyers**

BOARD**SOURCE**®

Building Effective Nonprofit Boards

Library of Congress Cataloging-in-Publication Data

Moyers, Richard L.

  The nonprofit chief executive's ten basic responsibilities / Rick
Moyers. -- 2nd ed.

    p. cm.

  ISBN 1-58686-130-1

1. Nonprofit organizations--Management. 2. Chief executive
officers. 3. Leadership. I. BoardSource (Organization) II. Title.

  HD62.6.M69 2012

  658.4'2--dc23

          2012016277

Published by BoardSource
750 9th Street, NW, Suite 650
Washington, DC 20001

BOARDSOURCE®
Building Effective Nonprofit Boards

BoardSource is dedicated to advancing the public good by building exceptional nonprofit boards and inspiring board service.

BoardSource was established in 1988 by the Association of Governing Boards of Universities and Colleges (AGB) and Independent Sector (IS). Prior to this, in the early 1980s, the two organizations had conducted a survey and found that although 30 percent of respondents believed they were doing a good job of board education and training, the rest of the respondents reported little, if any, activity in strengthening governance. As a result, AGB and IS proposed the creation of a new organization whose mission would be to increase the effectiveness of nonprofit boards.

With a lead grant from the Kellogg Foundation and funding from five other donors, BoardSource opened its doors in 1988 as the National Center for Nonprofit Boards with a staff of three and an operating budget of $385,000. On January 1, 2002, BoardSource took on its new name and identity. These changes were the culmination of an extensive process of understanding how we were perceived, what our audiences wanted, and how we could best meet the needs of nonprofit organizations.

Today, BoardSource is the premier voice of nonprofit governance. Its highly acclaimed products, programs, and services mobilize boards so that organizations fulfill their missions, achieve their goals, increase their impact, and extend their influence. BoardSource is a 501(c)(3) organization.

BoardSource provides

- resources to nonprofit leaders through workshops, training, and an extensive Web site (www.boardsource.org)

- governance consultants who work directly with nonprofit leaders to design specialized solutions to meet an organization's needs

- the world's largest, most comprehensive selection of material on nonprofit governance, including a large selection of books and toolkits

- an annual conference that brings together approximately 900 governance experts, board members, and chief executives and senior staff from around the world

For more information, please visit our Web site at www. boardsource.org, e-mail us at mail@boardsource.org, or call us at 800-883-6262.

Have You Used These BoardSource Resources?

THE GOVERNANCE SERIES

1. *Ten Basic Responsibilities of Nonprofit Boards, Second Edition*
2. *Legal Responsibilities of Nonprofit Boards, Second Edition*
3. *Financial Responsibilities of Nonprofit Boards, Second Edition*
4. *Fundraising Responsibilities of Nonprofit Boards, Second Edition*
5. *The Nonprofit Board's Role in Mission, Planning, and Evaluation, Second Edition*
6. *Structures and Practices of Nonprofit Boards, Second Edition*

OTHER PUBLICATIONS

Chief Executive Transitions: How to Hire and Support a Nonprofit CEO

Nonprofit Executive Compensation: Planning, Performance, and Pay, Second Edition

Chief Executive Succession Planning: Essential Guidance for Boards and CEOs, Second Edition

The Board Chair Handbook, Second Edition

Taming the Troublesome Board Member

Culture of Inquiry: Healthy Debate in the Boardroom

Governance as Leadership: Reframing the Work of Nonprofit Boards

The Board Building Cycle: Nine Steps to Finding, Recruiting, and Engaging Nonprofit Board Members, Second Edition

The Source: Twelve Principles of Governance That Power Exceptional Boards

Fearless Fundraising for Nonprofit Boards, Second Edition

Govern Green: Driving Your Organization's Commitment to Sustainability

Who's Minding the Money? An Investment Guide for Nonprofit Board Members, Seeoond Edition

The Handbook of Nonprofit Governance

Meeting, and Exceeding Expectations: A Guide to Successful Nonprofit Board Meetings, Second Edition

Understanding Nonprofit Financial Statements, Third Edition

The Nonprofit Dashboard: A Tool for Tracking Progress

Better Bylaws; Creating Effective Rules for Your Nonprofit Board, Second Edition

Managing Conflicts of Interest: A Primer for Nonprofit Boards, Second Edition

The Nonprofit Policy Sampler, Second Edition

Driving Strategic Planning: A Nonprofit Executive's Guide, Second Edition

Trouble at the Top: The Nonprofit Board's Guide to Managing an Imperfect Chief Executive

Navigating the Organizational Lifecycle: A Capacity-Building Guide for Nonprofit Leaders

Building the Governance Partnership: The Chief Executive's Guide to Getting the Best from the Board, Second Edition

The Nonprofit Board Answer Book: A Practical Guide for Board Members and Chief Executives, Third Edition

Govern More, Manage Less: Harnessing the Power of Your Nonprofit Board, Second Edition

DVDs

Meeting the Challenge: An Orientation to Nonprofit Board Service
Speaking of Money: A Guide to Fundraising for Nonprofit Board Members

ONLINE ASSESSMENTS

Board Self-Assessment
Assessment of the Chief Executive
Executive Search — Needs Assessment

CERTIFICATE PROGRAMS

Certificate of Nonprofit Board Education
Leadership Certificate for Nonprofit Chief Executives
Leadership Certificate for Nonprofit Board Chairs

For an up-to-date list of publications and information about current prices, membership, and other services, please call BoardSource at 800-883-6262 or visit our Web site at www.boardsource.org. For consulting services, please e-mail us at consulting@boardsource.org or call 877-892-6293.

CONTENTS

INTRODUCTION

A job announcement or help-wanted advertisement for the typical nonprofit chief executive[1] position might read something like this:

> *Nonprofit organization seeks talented and visionary leader with a program expertise, a commitment to its mission, management and supervisory skills, and financial acumen. Position also requires strong communication skills, including writing and public speaking. The successful candidate will be responsible for closing a significant annual gap between the organization's financial resources and the work it hopes to do, and must be willing to be supervised by a group of volunteers whose role is loosely defined and whose composition changes regularly.*

The list of qualifications and desired attributes in nonprofit chief executives is often much longer, and may include professional certifications and advanced degrees, a successful fundraising track record, a background in business or government, or experience in advocacy and lobbying. When reading through these lists, one almost expects to run across "faster than a speeding bullet" and "able to leap tall buildings in a single bound." Such announcements also usually omit a few items, such as a willingness to earn less than comparable professionals in business or government, or skill at juggling cash flow while the organization is waiting for delayed payments.

Despite the breadth of skills required, the complexity of the job, and the growing challenges facing many nonprofit organizations, hundreds of thousands of leaders have stepped into the chief executive role, and through their work are making extraordinary contributions to communities across the United States and around the world.

---

1   Executive director and president are the two most common titles for the chief staff position in a nonprofit organization. This book uses the more generic term, chief executive.

Chief executives' professional backgrounds are as varied as the organizations they lead. Some are the founders of their organizations and have developed their own skills and knowledge as their organizations have grown. Many have spent their entire careers in the nonprofit sector; others migrated from business or government. They are attorneys, social workers, psychologists, accountants, doctors, nurses, teachers, and artists. Few began their careers intending to lead a nonprofit organization.

Although an increasing number of nonprofit employees have degrees in nonprofit management, most undergraduate and graduate programs are not designed specifically to train people to be nonprofit chief executives. In addition, most chief executives are in the role for the first time.[2] They come to their jobs with strong skills and experience in some aspects of the role. The rest they learn on the job, with few obvious places to turn for support.

In contrast, nonprofit boards have abundant resources for clarifying their roles and strengthening their performances. Over the past two decades, dozens of books, self-assessments, and toolkits have been developed to help board members understand their responsibilities. Over the same time period, very little has been produced specifically for chief executives. Many authors and researchers acknowledge that the board and chief executive share responsibility for governance, yet most of the available literature and tools focus on the board. This leaves the chief executive in the position of someone trying to complete a crossword puzzle with only the clues for across.

Since the relationship with the board looms large in the life of every nonprofit chief executive and confusion over respective roles is rampant, this book was created as a companion to *Ten Basic Responsibilities of Nonprofit Boards* (BoardSource, 2009) to examine the chief executive's responsibilities through the same lens as those of the board. It discusses all the chief executive's responsibilities, including supervising the staff, overseeing operations, and leading the senior management team. These general management

---

2   Bell, Jeanne, Richard Moyers, and Timothy Wolfred. Daring to Lead 2006: A National Study of Nonprofit Executive Leadership. San Francisco: CompassPoint Nonprofit Services and the Meyer Foundation, 2006.

responsibilities, which are not linked directly to the partnership with the board, comprise a large and important portion of the chief executive's job. Chief executives who want to improve their skills as supervisors, communicators, or program managers can draw on many resources, including business literature and continuing education programs. Chief executives who want to understand their responsibilities in the context of their partnership with the board have many fewer places to turn. This book seeks to fill that gap.

This publication draws on a variety of sources, including the work of many authors, conversations with hundreds of chief executives over nearly two decades, and several recent national surveys of executives and boards. It is intended primarily for chief executives — for those who are new to the role and for more seasoned executives who want to improve. Board members, other nonprofit staff, and grantmakers can also use this book to better understand the chief executive's role.

THE CHIEF EXECUTIVE AND THE BOARD

The role of the nonprofit chief executive has evolved over the past century for a variety of reasons, including the growth and complexity of the nonprofit sector, the increasing professionalism and specialization of nonprofit employees, and other changes in the paid and volunteer work force.

The models or frameworks discussed below are rooted in that evolution. They offer competing and sometimes contradictory ideas about the role of the chief executive and how executives and board members should interact.

- *Strong board, subordinate executive.* This leadership model was once much more common than it is today, although many board members and chief executives still believe that the chief executive falls below the board in the organization's hierarchy and that the board's role is to supervise and control the executive in much the same way that any manager supervises a subordinate. Some organizations go through a period of strong board leadership with a relatively weak executive as part of their evolution and growth. Under this model the executive is somewhat passive and looks to the board for leadership and initiative. The board is likely to be involved in all major management decisions. One drawback is that board members may not have the information or expertise to make needed decisions. Executives also sometimes express frustration that the board is holding the organization back or will not let them make needed changes. Often these chief executives don't believe they have a role in changing the situation.

- *Strong executive, ornamental board.* This model is increasingly common, often because a talented and charismatic chief executive has a clear vision for the organization. Sometimes these executives are founders; sometimes they have taken over the organization during a difficult period or led it to unprecedented success. Organizations that operate this way can be successful and even effective. The drawback is that the executive holds almost absolute power. The potential for disaster is high, and even in the best cases the board is seldom used to its full potential as an asset.

- *Equal partners.* Several authors, including Cyril Houle and Peter Drucker, have written about the board and the executive as partners or colleagues who work collaboratively to achieve common goals. This is perhaps the least controversial but most ambiguous conception of the relationship between the chief executive and the board. It argues for flexibility and cooperation, but at the same time provides much opportunity for disagreement and confusion.

- *Partners with clear boundaries.* To reduce ambiguity, the well-known writer John Carver has urged clearer thinking. The Carver model of governance includes the concept of "executive limitations." Boards are urged to define in clear terms everything the executive is not allowed to do. Inside that fence, the executive has complete latitude to manage the organization. Many nonprofit executives, particularly those who have suffered from micromanaging boards, have found Carver's ideas helpful. Some argue that this framework sacrifices flexibility for the sake of clarity.

- *Servant-leaders.* Robert Greenleaf, an educator and retired corporate executive, coined the phrase "servant-leadership" in the early 1970s to describe the belief that people should first seek to serve and then lead as a way to expand their service to individuals and institutions. Servant-leadership encourages collaboration, trust, empathy, and the ethical use of power. Executives and board members who approach leadership from this perspective might, at least in theory, find themselves less preoccupied with who's really in charge and more focused on how best to help each other and the organization.

Each of these ideas about the role of the chief executive has merit, is right in some respects, and claims many adherents. None offers a completely accurate view of the chief executive's role or a sure-fire recipe for the success of the chief executive and the organization. However, these different perspectives provide important context for any discussion of the chief executive's role and help explain why boards and chief executives sometimes reach very different conclusions about how they should do their jobs.

UNDERLYING ASSUMPTIONS

Following essentially the same outline as *Ten Basic Responsibilities of Nonprofit Boards,* this publication lays out the chief executive's broad responsibilities, often in the context of the partnership with the board, based on four underlying assumptions.

1. The role and responsibilities of the chief executive vary widely depending on an organization's size, structure, and history. There is no one "right" role for the chief executive and no standard position description that is applicable to all organizations.

2. The line of demarcation between the board's responsibilities and those of the chief executive is imprecise. Occasionally it's invisible. This book does not attempt to draw sharp and impractical distinctions between the board's role and that of the executive. Instead, it emphasizes the importance of creating clear expectations and a shared understanding of the mutually supportive and complementary roles of the board and the chief executive.

3. An effective partnership between board and chief executive requires a balance of power and authority. The board must have enough power and independence to carry out its legal responsibilities and to supervise the executive. The chief executive needs adequate authority to manage the organization and exercise leadership in the broader community. Finding and maintaining that balance is one of the central challenges of executive leadership.

4. Even within a single organization, the role of the chief executive changes over time based on shared history and trust, changing skills and personalities on the board, the growth and professional development of the chief executive, and other factors. Chief executives who recognize that their role is not static and who embrace and plan for inevitable changes in their role are more likely to be successful.

Scholars Robert Herman and Richard Heimovics described the role of the chief executive as containing "strange loops and tangled hierarchies."[3] Chief executives have many responsibilities that are distinct from those of the board and also manage many other important partnerships — with staff, donors, public officials, and leaders of other nonprofits. Because the chief executive's job is so complicated, it cannot be easily captured in a tidy 10-point checklist. The 10 sections that follow attempt to acknowledge the breadth and complexity of the chief executive's role and can serve as benchmarks and guideposts for those chief executives who want to explore specific aspects of their responsibilities in greater depth.

---

3   Herman, Robert D. and Richard D. Heimovics. Executive Leadership in Nonprofit Organizations: New Strategies for Shaping Board-Staff Dynamics. San Francisco: Jossey-Bass, 1991.

CHAPTER 1
Commit to the Mission

First and foremost, the chief executive should have a thorough understanding of the organization's mission, programs, and the context in which it operates. The most effective executives go beyond simply understanding the mission. They are deeply committed to the organization and its work. They care enough about the mission to motivate themselves and others to work hard to accomplish the organization's goals.

In theory, the board holds ultimate responsibility for determining the organization's mission and purpose. In practice, most chief executives wield considerable influence. Many board members state explicitly that they expect the chief executive to supply a vision for the organization's future around which the board can rally and mobilize. Such visionary executives often also have strong ideas about how the mission should evolve.

Whether or not they provide the vision, chief executives are responsible for keeping the mission at the forefront when making decisions about staffing, allocation of resources, and competing priorities. Chief executives are also responsible for monitoring trends in the field, changes in community needs, and other information about the organization's work that can inform discussions about whether the mission needs to be shifted or fine-tuned.

The term "mission drift" is often used to describe the gradual accretion of programs and activities that may not directly support the organization's core mission or priorities. Entrepreneurial chief executives, donors with very specific ideas, and board members with individual agendas all can contribute to mission drift. The danger is that off-mission programs and activities, even when worthwhile and well funded, distract an organization from its critical activities and challenges.

The chief executive should be the primary guardian against mission drift. A skilled executive will make sure the board gets the information it needs to have periodic, well-informed conversations about mission, and that the staff and other stakeholders, including grantmakers, have a clear sense of the organization's mission and can distinguish between activities and programs that are essential and those that are tangential and opportunistic.

Chief executives who are founders have particular advantages and challenges around mission. Their advantage is a deep understanding of the mission and a strong commitment to it. Their challenge is to acknowledge the board's ultimate authority over mission, recognizing that the board has the power to redefine the mission — and even hire a new executive — if necessary. Some founders are never able to take that step, which is essential for the longevity of the organization and the long-term strength of the board.

Occasionally a chief executive will accept a position with the belief that the organization's mission needs to change, or reach that conclusion after some time on the job. Even if that executive is the founder, and even if his or her instinct is right, a decision about mission is a decision for the board. An organization is unlikely to succeed if the board and the chief executive have a persistent disagreement about mission. An effective executive will either find a way to bring the board around or realize that the board holds all the trump cards and move on.

Key Questions

- Have we articulated our mission in a way that inspires and motivates both the executive and the board? If not, what steps could we take to refresh the mission and renew everyone's commitment?

- Does all the work of our organization directly support our mission? If not, are there things we could stop doing, or work that could be handed off to another organization?

- Can everyone on the board recite a reasonably accurate version of our mission? How can we use the board materials and board meetings to help both the board and the executive connect more strongly to the mission?

- Do the day-to-day responsibilities of the chief executive provide enough opportunities to re-connect to the mission? For many executives, maintaining that connection is essential to avoid burnout and maintain motivation and focus.

CHAPTER 2
Lead the Staff and Manage the Organization

This broad responsibility is the core of the chief executive's job.

The board is responsible for hiring the chief executive, assessing his or her performance, and deciding when a new leader is needed. Except in unusual circumstances, the chief executive is ultimately responsible for hiring and managing the rest of the staff, making sure programs are well run, and ensuring an adequate management infrastructure.

In large organizations, executives may delegate some of their management responsibilities to a senior management team, specialists in finance, technology, and human resources, or outside consultants. In many community-based nonprofits, the executive handles a wide array of management responsibilities directly with little or no additional administrative support.

No matter how they are delegated, the chief executive's management responsibilities include

- *Hiring, managing, and supervising the staff.* Staff salaries represent the single largest category of spending for most organizations, and staff members are essential to the delivery of programs and services or otherwise carrying out the organization's work. Although the chief executive may delegate hiring responsibility to other managers, the executive is ultimately responsible and accountable to the board for hiring and managing the staff. One of the regrets most often cited by successful, long-tenured chief executives is that they sometimes allowed difficult personnel situations to drag on for too long before making the decision to fire an employee — an important reminder that the responsibility for hiring and managing employees sometimes leads to the need to make difficult decisions, and that a failure to act can damage an organization.

- *Inspiring and motivating employees.* This involves both leadership and management skills, including helping all staff members understand how their work supports the organization's larger mission and goals, taking the time to celebrate success, and maintaining an optimistic outlook even when the organization faces serious challenges.

- *Promoting a culture that reflects the organization's values, encourages good performance, and rewards productivity.* Culture is the set of attitudes, norms, beliefs, and customs that add up to an organization's personality. Over time, the chief executive has more power than anyone else to shape culture, including how decisions are made, how the organization recognizes achievements and corrects failures, how staff members communicate, or how meetings are typically run. An organization's culture will inevitably emerge over time even if the chief executive has not given the matter any direct thought. An effective chief executive will pay attention to culture and work intentionally to create a culture that supports the mission.

- *Creating a staff structure that supports the organization's goals, objectives, and priorities.* Organizational structures, including allocation of staff responsibilities and lines of authority and accountability, vary based on organizational size and mission. All chief executives should periodically examine the staff structure to make sure it meets the organization's management needs. Because situations vary so widely, prescriptions and formulas are difficult. However, some themes are common throughout the nonprofit sector. Many small and mid-sized organizations have relatively flat structures, with a large number of employees reporting directly to the chief executive. This can leave the chief executive swamped with internal details and unable to focus on supporting the board or building external relationships. It can also concentrate almost all decision-making responsibility with the chief executive, making it difficult for other staff members to develop their own management and leadership skills. Whatever the structure, it needs to be flexible enough to accommodate the strengths and diverse talents of individual employees, and it should provide opportunities for senior staff members and lower level employees to develop their skills.

- *Ensuring that employees have the work environment, supplies, and equipment needed to do their jobs efficiently.* By serving as a champion for adequate technology, equipment that works, and an office environment that encourages efficiency and professionalism, the chief executive can help keep employees satisfied and productive. Because so many nonprofits are operating with inadequate resources, chief executives may experience sticker shock when facing software upgrades or leasing office space. When considering such investments, executives should think about the impact on efficiency and productivity, staff morale, and quality of service. If the chief executive doesn't believe that infrastructure matters, the organization is unlikely to spend money on upgrades. Long-term neglect can cripple an organization.

- *Offering salaries and benefit packages that will attract and retain qualified staff members.* The same pressures that lead organizations to under-invest in technology and other infrastructure often lead to low staff salaries and extremely limited benefits packages. While an organization needs to operate within the resources it has available, chief executives should ask themselves whether current salary levels hamper the organization's ability to hire high potential employees or senior managers who could help improve the organization's performance and generate additional resources. Significant changes in salary levels and employee benefits require leadership from the chief executive.

- *Supporting the growth and development of existing staff members.* Staff members who feel that their abilities and potential are recognized, who have the opportunity to take on challenging assignments and increased responsibilities, and who can develop their skills by attending conferences and trainings will usually be more satisfied with their jobs and invested in the organization's success. The chief executive can provide leadership in this area by creating a culture that supports employee growth, by protecting professional development budgets when finances are tight, and by providing opportunities for internal advancement.

- *Ensuring the quality, efficiency, and effectiveness of programs and services.* This aspect of the chief executive's role is discussed in more detail in Chapter 9. In short, the chief executive is ultimately responsible for delivering on promises made to clients or patrons, funders, and the community. This includes developing ways to measure performance, gathering data and using it to improve programs and services, thinking critically about how resources are allocated, and periodically engaging the board in conversations about program effectiveness.

- *Leading by example.* The chief executive's actions and attitude resonate throughout the organization. The executive who works 60-hour weeks and never takes vacation, cuts ethical corners, or makes disparaging remarks about board members and colleagues will be observed and eventually imitated by staff members. Demonstrating — and encouraging — an appropriate work-life balance, modeling ethical behavior, and setting a positive and professional tone for the organization are critical, and often overlooked, responsibilities.

In small organizations, the chief executive may choose to involve board members or even the board as a whole in some areas of management. This may sometimes be an effective use of board members' time and expertise, but it also has the potential to create problems. For example, involving the board in one hiring decision implies additional future involvement. And using board members as expert volunteers can create confusion about whether they are acting on behalf of the board. Chief executives should exercise caution about using the board and board members as management consultants. Such involvement should generally be initiated by the chief executive, not by the board, and the executive should be very clear about what the board is being asked to do (serve as a sounding board, or make a decision) and why help is needed.

MYTHS ABOUT THE RESPONSIBILITIES OF THE BOARD AND MANAGEMENT

Two of the most popular adages about the division of management responsibility between board and executive are less than helpful, if not downright misleading.

1. *The board has only one employee.* The board's one employee is the chief executive, and this simple maxim is often invoked to reinforce the executive's authority over the staff and to discourage the board from meddling in hiring, staff performance evaluations, and decisions on employee promotions and individual compensation. This statement is not literally true but not quite false either. All employees

work for the organization, and the board retains ultimate responsibility and liability for employment relationships. If a chief executive terminates an employee who then takes legal action, the board will quickly discover that it does have more than one employee. For that reason, the chief executive will want to keep the board informed about consequential decisions and may even want to seek the board's counsel and approval. Similarly, when hiring an employee or consultant who will have significant interaction with the board, the executive may want to involve the board or individual board members in the interview and selection process. And when an employee has a serious complaint about the chief executive, such as malfeasance or other inappropriate behavior, board involvement is almost inevitable (although the board should proceed with extreme caution). In short, a line between the board's responsibilities and the chief executive's authority does exist, but is less clear than conventional wisdom suggests.

2. *The board governs; the staff manages.* This formulation and its variants are frequently cited to help distinguish the board's role from that of the staff. In general, management is the responsibility of the chief executive and the staff. Governance is a shared responsibility of the board and the chief executive. But the board does manage now and then, such as when it evaluates the chief executive's performance and determines compensation. And individual board members often help with management tasks. The chief executive is certainly the organization's lead manager, but also governs in partnership with the board.

Many of the responsibilities and tasks mentioned briefly in this section are discussed in greater detail on the pages that follow.

KEY QUESTIONS

- Are the building blocks in place to support the executive in making difficult personnel decisions? For example, are employment policies up to date and well documented, are employee performance reviews conducted regularly, and do the executive and board have access to legal counsel?

- Does our organization's management and staffing structure provide adequate support to the chief executive, allowing the executive to focus on critical responsibilities — such as fundraising and working with the board — that can't be handled by anyone else?

- How would an outsider describe our organization's culture? Is there a disconnect between our organization's culture and its mission and values?

CHAPTER 3
Exercise Responsible Financial Stewardship

The chief executive is responsible for making sound day-to-day and month-to-month financial decisions within the parameters established by the board.

Chief executives do not need all the skills of a bookkeeper or a certified public accountant, but they do need a solid understanding of the basic principles of finance and accounting. Even if the organization uses an external accountant or bookkeeper, employs a chief financial officer, or has a board treasurer who plays a hands-on role in monitoring the organization's finances, the chief executive should be able to explain the organization's budget and interpret its financial statements to board members, funders, and other stakeholders. The chief executive should also understand the organization's budget and financial statements well enough to use them as management and decision-making tools and to instinctively spot errors and inconsistencies before they are presented to the board or circulated outside the organization.

Chief executives should be able to make smart decisions based on the organization's overall financial picture. Three areas in which executives (and by extension nonprofit boards) often fall short are monitoring the organization's cash flow, developing and maintaining adequate operating reserves, and understanding trends in income and expense over time.

Nonprofits that own property, equipment, and other nonliquid assets — or those whose income arrives in large seasonal chunks — may sometimes run short on cash even when they meet their budget projections and their balance sheets are healthy. These moments of crisis can be demoralizing and disruptive and can only be avoided by monitoring cash flow separately and in addition to performance against budget. Adequate cash flow planning requires timely preparation of bank reconciliations and internal financial statements as well as planning and monitoring tools that are distinct from those used to track performance against budget or to prepare financial statements.

Operating reserves are another often neglected tool that can help nonprofit organizations achieve financial stability. In effect, operating reserves are savings accounts that nonprofits can use to weather unanticipated financial turbulence or make important one-time investments that fall outside the normal budget. Unlike endowments, operating reserves are not restricted and can be used for current needs. Operating reserves can help nonprofits manage short-term cash flow and can be used to cover an operating deficit if the board and executive believe a deficit is necessary.

Most financial management experts recommend that organizations maintain operating reserves equivalent to at least three months' worth of expenses, while acknowledging that for many organizations, higher levels would be prudent. Several recent studies have shown that a majority of nonprofits don't have three months of reserves, and many have no reserves at all.

Nonprofits without reserves face the same financial risks as people with no savings. The loss of a major grant, a leaky roof that needs to be replaced, or a delayed reimbursement on a large contract can throw the organization into crisis. Organizations without reserves are also often unable to take advantage of opportunities for growth or expansion because they are unable to tolerate any financial risk.

Many boards are understandably wary of accumulating money for reserves, fearing that the organization will undermine its position with potential donors by appearing too rich, and believing that they have an obligation to spend as much money as possible on current programs. Many board members don't recognize the distinction between reserves and an endowment, and may not understand why reserves are important.

Working in partnership with the treasurer, the chief executive is responsible for educating the board about operating reserves and helping the board develop a target level of reserves and policies that govern their use. The chief executive is also responsible for proposing a budget that will help achieve the target level within a timeframe that the board feels is reasonable. Without some leadership from the executive, the critical issue of operating reserves is likely to be neglected.

Developing adequate operating reserves is not the work of a single year. The most common way organizations build reserves is by consistently operating at a modest surplus over many years. Building reserves requires a longer-term focus than many chief executives bring to their financial management role.

Unfortunately, many nonprofit executives approach their financial management responsibilities with a short-term focus. They are preoccupied with the current year's budget or this month's cash flow and too seldom take the time to reflect on trends of the past three to five years and their implications for the future. This short-term focus, while understandable, is also shortsighted. Last year's deficit will affect this year's cash flow, even if things have since improved. Developing operating reserves, building an endowment, and maintaining and operating a facility all require a longer planning horizon. Because board leadership and overall board composition change frequently, the board is unlikely to take a long view unless prompted and provided with the right information by the chief executive.

The chief executive helps the board carry out all its financial responsibilities, which include approving the annual budget, reviewing and accepting the external audit, and monitoring financial performance throughout the year. The chief executive is responsible for presenting the annual budget and interim financial statements in a timely and accurate manner for review and action by the board, and for making sure that the audit proceeds on schedule and that the organization can provide information and documentation needed by the auditor.

In many cases, particularly in larger organizations, a chief financial officer plays a critical role in managing the organization's finances and presenting financial information to the board — especially when the chief executive has limited financial management experience. This requires a close working partnership between the chief financial officer and the chief executive, who remains ultimately accountable to the board for the organization's financial performance. In situations where chief executives have limited financial expertise or lack confidence in their abilities, an important part of the chief financial officer's role is to build the executive's skills and capacity, rather than developing an independent relationship with the board around financial issues.

Interaction between the chief executive and the board around financial matters can take a variety of forms. Some boards rubber-stamp a recommended budget or accept the audit with little or no discussion. Others ask detailed questions about individual budget line items. Some middle ground is probably most appropriate, and the chief executive is responsible for ensuring that the board's role in financial oversight is meaningful, not perfunctory.

The chief executive is responsible for working with board leadership to determine how the board should be involved in budget development, what level of detail the board needs so it can make sense of financial statements, how the board will interact with the external auditor, and what role the chief financial officer and the board treasurer or finance committee chair will play in board meetings. As a general rule, the staff is better equipped to develop the budget than the board, and boards should be discouraged from micromanaging. However, the board's ownership of the budget, in partnership with management, is key to board engagement in fundraising. Board members who do not understand the budget or suspect that the organization wastes money won't be enthusiastic fundraisers.

Chief executives who whittle the board's participation in budgeting and financial monitoring down to a bare minimum are likely to meet little resistance, since most boards find financial matters mysterious and perplexing. But such chief executives should not be surprised to find themselves standing alone on the edge of a precipice when financial projections fall short and more money is urgently needed.

In addition to helping the board exercise its fiduciary responsibilities, the executive should think carefully about how the staff is involved in budgeting and financial management. Staff members who understand the budget and the organization's financial situation are more likely to act as responsible financial stewards. Involving senior staff in budgeting and financial management is also a way to develop future leadership within the organization. Program staff members may have limited understanding of financial management and accounting concepts, and they will need to develop those skills to move into senior nonprofit leadership positions.

Finally, the chief executive plays an important role in protecting the organization's assets against fraud and abuse and monitoring the appropriate use of resources. This includes ensuring that the organization has sound internal financial controls, implementing changes recommended by the auditor, and making sure the organization has adequate insurance protection and appropriate risk management policies.

The chief executive's responsibility also includes more subjective judgments about the appropriateness of expenditures. Executives are especially vulnerable to criticisms or perceived improprieties related to their own expenditures, such as credit card payments for travel and entertainment, office parties, or gifts. A wise chief executive will consider how such expenses might look to outsiders and will make sure that policies and procedures are in place to protect the organization's assets and reputation and that they are scrupulously followed.

KEY QUESTIONS

- Do the chief executive and board regularly receive timely and informative financial reports and projections that help them make decisions? If not, why not, and what immediate steps could we take to address the problem?

- Do we have adequate operating reserves or a realistic plan for building our reserves?

- If a major donor were to offer us an unexpected gift of one million dollars, do we know how we would use that money?

CHAPTER 4
Lead and Manage Fundraising

For nonprofit organizations that rely on charitable contributions from private sources, perhaps no area of chief executive responsibility causes more anxiety, hand wringing, and buck passing than fundraising. Most executives are dissatisfied with their board's involvement in fundraising, wish they had a larger development staff, and yearn for an income-producing endowment or stronger earned income streams that would relieve their ongoing worries about fundraising.

The division of responsibilities around fundraising will vary widely based on an organization's size, the relative importance of contributed income, and the types of funding that the organization receives. One principle does hold true for most organizations, from universities to homeless shelters: The chief executive is one of the most important participants in building relationships with key individual and institutional donors and ensuring effective board involvement in fundraising.

Deep involvement in fundraising is usually an inescapable part of the chief executive's job. Several factors contribute to this reality:

- Institutional funders, such as foundations and corporations, often make giving decisions based on their confidence in the chief executive's leadership. In addition, many funders want to meet with someone who has extensive knowledge of all the organization's programs. Particularly in community-based nonprofits, but also in many others, this means the chief executive is the best person to build relationships with funders.

- The most effective solicitor is someone whom the potential contributor views as a peer. In some cases, this may be a board member; in many others, it will be the chief executive. Having an opportunity to meet with the chief executive and to hear first-hand from the organization's top leader about challenges and exciting new programs helps donors feel that their support is important. Even if the donor does not view the chief executive as a peer, the executive is often the next best thing — the person in charge. Development staff can be invaluable in cultivation and solicitation, but the involvement of the organization's top board and staff leaders is essential in working with major donors.

• Even in organizations with talented development staff, engaging the board of directors in fundraising is difficult without the support and involvement of the chief executive, who influences the board's agenda and focus. If the chief executive seems uninterested or uninvolved in fundraising, even the most charismatic and motivational development director or consultant will have trouble convincing board members that their participation matters.

As one of the organization's lead fundraisers and the person who has the broadest perspective on the organization and all its components, the executive should be able to speak compellingly and convincingly about why the organization needs donor support. As a general rule, this case for support should focus on the needs of the community or the people the organization serves, not the needs of the organization.

In addition to their direct role in raising money, chief executives are responsible for helping the board focus its attention on fundraising strategy and policy. Topics for discussion might include a gift acceptance policy, strategies for diversification of funding sources, or cost-effectiveness of fundraising efforts. The approval of policy is clearly the board's responsibility, but in most cases the chief executive points out the need for board action or discussion, works with the board chair or a committee chair to frame the discussion, and drafts the policy or proposes alternatives. An ever-present danger is that the board or the resource development committee spends all its time talking about policy and doesn't raise any money.

Chief executives, especially those of smaller organizations, are often put in the awkward position of making sure that all board members have made an annual financial contribution. Even in situations where the board has approved a policy stating that all members are expected to contribute and a board leader has reminded members of this expectation, achieving full participation may require ongoing reminders and a few awkward conversations. Sometimes a polite and friendly nudge from the chief executive or development officer may keep things on track. In most cases, a board leader, rather than the chief executive or a member of the development staff, should champion the effort to make sure all board members follow through on their commitments. The chief executive may still need to nudge the board member who's leading the charge on board contributions and should make sure that person has the information he or she needs to follow up with board members about their gifts.

The chief executive's leadership role in fundraising is broad and also varies widely from organization to organization. Often, the chief executive leads the board and staff in identifying fundraising strategies that are right for the organization's mission and stage of development, and in facilitating the involvement of individual board members in the solicitation process. As the leader of the staff, the chief executive is responsible for allocating enough staff and other resources (including technology) to get the job done, holding staff members accountable for work plans and results, keeping the board updated on progress, and making sure promises to funders are kept. Development staff and board committees often play an important supporting role, but the chief executive is almost always the linchpin.

KEY QUESTIONS

- Are fundraising responsibilities included in our chief executive's job description, and have the board and chief executive worked together to develop realistic shared expectations for fundraising — including how board members will be involved in supporting fundraising?

- Do we have a policy requiring individual board member contributions, and does someone on the board have clear responsibility for soliciting those gifts?

- Do we have adequate staff to achieve our fundraising goals, and do we have the software and other tools staff members need to be successful?

CHAPTER 5
Follow the Highest Ethical Standards, Ensure Accountability, and Comply with the Law

The chief executive handles the concrete aspects of the organization's compliance with legal and regulatory requirements. The executive supervises staff members or consultants who prepare and file required government documents, implement human resources policies, make sure that payroll taxes are paid and withheld, follow internal financial controls, prepare annual reports, and handle a host of other small details that, taken together, add up to an accountable and well-managed organization.

Even though the board of directors is responsible for ensuring ethics and accountability, the board will have a difficult if not impossible time fulfilling its responsibility without the cooperation and active participation of the chief executive. As an example, the external audit gives the board an annual spot-check in some areas but does not examine every financial transaction in detail. An audit might tell the board that the staff hadn't followed proper check-signing policies but would not offer an opinion about whether the staff's behavior was ethical and consistent with the organization's values. The responsibility for educating the board about ethics and accountability, pointing out areas of vulnerability, developing policies for board approval, and ensuring day-to-day compliance falls primarily to the chief executive.

Without a common framework or a shared set of expectations, discussions of ethics are subjective and illusory. Behaving ethically goes beyond simply avoiding illegal behavior; most nonprofits aspire to a higher standard. Questions of honesty, confidentiality, equity, due process, conflicting or competing interests, and nepotism arise frequently in the life of a chief executive and constitute a vast gray area with the potential to damage an organization and its executive.

Too few boards have honest discussions about these issues, and ethics and conflict-of-interest policies, when they are adopted, often fail to exorcise the elephant in the room. Further, without some prompting and guidance from the chief executive — as with many of the areas discussed in this publication — the board won't initiate such a conversation on its own.

In framing discussions of ethics and accountability, the chief executive may ask the board for affirmation of existing policies or guidance on new policies that govern

- practices and behaviors that are illegal and will not be tolerated under any circumstances

- problems outside the organization that have the potential to damage the organization, such as criminal charges against a key employee or board member

- issues within the organization, such as nepotism or questionable expenditures that, while not illegal, might trigger problems or cause others to question the organization's integrity

- guidelines about behavior that relate to the organization's core values

In each case, the board and executive should develop written policies that clarify unacceptable behavior and provide the board and executive with tools to use when problems arise. Compliance rests squarely on the shoulders of the chief executive.

The chief executive's values and behavior set the tone for the rest of the organization, and boards have a specific responsibility for ensuring the ethics and accountability of chief executives, since they function with no other supervisor and relatively few checks and balances.

Given the quantity, frequency, and nature of financial scandals that have plagued the nonprofit sector over the past two decades, boards should pay special attention to chief executives' expenditures for travel, entertainment, and other reimbursements. In small organizations, the board chair or treasurer will probably want to approve checks made out to the chief executive, as well as the chief executive's expense reports and credit card transactions. In larger nonprofits, boards should make sure they understand how such expenditures are authorized and the underlying policies that govern spending.

In organizations where the board has no involvement in reviewing or approving chief executive expenditures, the executive should ask for new policies and procedures. To some chief executives, this type of board involvement may seem intrusive. However, early intrusive board involvement is preferable to after-the-fact disagreements about the appropriateness or reasonableness of expenditures or public embarrassment to the organization.

To preserve public confidence in nonprofit organizations, many nonprofit leaders have argued for greater transparency in the way nonprofits do business. The term transparency is often used in business and government to describe a way of doing business in which decision making, budgets, financial statements, and information about the organization's performance are open to the general public or to smaller groups of constituents and stakeholders. For businesses with shareholders and for some government bodies, this concept is relatively straightforward. For nonprofit organizations, the obligations of transparency are less clear-cut.

The assumption behind the push for transparency is that people who do business in glass houses are less prone to commit fraud or impropriety and more likely to act in the best interests of those who are watching from the outside. But glass houses also attract stone-throwers and peeping toms, and are more appropriate for some climates than others. The role of the chief executive is to help the board determine what level of transparency is right for the organization and its context.

KEY QUESTIONS

- Do we have in place the basic policies either required by law (a whistleblower policy, for example) or suggested by common sense (an anti-nepotism policy) to ensure that we adhere to the highest ethical standards?

- Does the board have a system in place for reviewing key policies and documents on an annual basis and to monitor our compliance with our own policies?

- Have the board and executive ever had a discussion about the organization's core values, and how those core values might translate into policies that guide ethical behavior?

- If the answer to any of these questions is no, how might the chief executive support the board in adopting better policies and monitoring compliance?

CHAPTER 6
Engage the Board in Planning and Lead Implementation

One of the most important governance responsibilities shared by the board and chief executive is ensuring that the organization has a solid plan for the future. This includes periodically revisiting the organization's mission and vision in light of changes in the community and the larger operating environment, making decisions about strategy and priorities for the future, ensuring that the organization's day-to-day activities are aligned with the vision and priorities, and understanding the plan's financial implications.

Fundamentally, the board, the chief executive, and the staff need to agree on a vision for the future and a course of action for taking the organization in that direction. Other stakeholders, such as funders or members, need to be assured that the organization is aware of its context and that its plans are reasonable and appropriate.

Stories of painful and pointless strategic planning processes have become part of the common folklore of the nonprofit sector, with "and then the plan just sat on the shelf, gathering dust" as the typical unhappy ending. Participating in a bad planning process is like acting in a play that is so long and so tedious that even the actors can't keep track of the plot. The chief executive holds primary responsibility for avoiding potential pitfalls and making sure the board and staff are engaged in a meaningful process.

The chief executive's role in planning includes

- *Recognizing the need for planning.* Because of their full-time involvement in the work of the organization, knowledge of peer organizations and community needs, and professional expertise, the chief executive and staff are often the first to recognize the need for planning. The expiration of an old plan is not necessarily justification for launching a new planning process unless other significant changes have occurred. Examples of developments that might trigger planning include the loss of a major program or funding stream, the emergence of a new organization that offers duplicative services, or shifts in government funding policies. A skillful executive will provide such information to the board consistently over time so that the need for planning doesn't come as a surprise. Once the chief executive believes that planning is needed, he or she will need buy-in from the board, beginning with the board chair and eventually having a discussion with the full board. The board will usually follow the executive's lead, although board members who have had a negative planning experience in the past may be reluctant to participate. Taking the time to listen to board members' concerns and letting the board help design an efficient process will help convince board members that their time will be well used.

- *Deciding how the board will participate.* In consultation with the board chair and possibly the full board, the chief executive needs to determine how best to involve the board in the process. Some board members will inevitably suggest that the staff simply develop a plan for board approval. While full board involvement may not be necessary, zero board involvement is not the right choice. Board members bring valuable skills and perspective, and at the end of the process the board needs to own and understand the plan. Some compromise — often a planning team that includes the board and staff, or full board involvement at certain stages in the process — is usually the best solution. With input from board members and in collaboration with the chair, the chief executive needs to propose a practical plan that engages the board without making unreasonable demands on board members' time or asking board members to participate in conversations for which they are ill suited.

- *Making planning a priority and allocating adequate resources.* If the chief executive is not willing to devote time and energy to the planning process, no one else in the organization is likely to do so. And without adequate staff support and attention to detail, the planning process will be unsatisfying and ultimately unsuccessful.

- *Giving the board some things to decide.* The planning process should give board members an opportunity to exercise leadership where it matters most — to discuss issues about which they have the background, expertise, and information to make decisions that will affect the organization's future. A laundry list of incremental shifts or a new phrase added to the mission statement won't fill the bill. The chief executive and the board chair or the chair of the planning committee should think carefully about how to frame the board's planning discussions and how the board's participation can be meaningful.

- *Creating mechanisms for implementation and monitoring progress.* This aspect of the chief executive's responsibility is essential to ensuring that the plan — however elegant or imaginative — does not become a neglected artifact. A meaningful strategic plan should lead to annual operating plans prepared by the chief executive and staff that include concrete tasks and measurable outcomes. The goals and objectives in the strategic plan should filter down into staff position descriptions, individual work plans, and performance reviews — including the board's review of the chief executive's performance. Chief executives need to exercise their authority as leaders and managers to ensure that the plan remains relevant to the organization's operations and that staff members are held accountable for their commitments. Chief executives should also use their partnership with the board chair to ensure that the plan remains relevant to the work of the board.

The practice of strategic planning varies widely and has continued to evolve over the past decade. As a result, many new tools and processes are available to help organizations develop strategy and plan for the future. However, this otherwise positive development has the potential to create confusion and disagreement among board members and between the board and the chief executive. Strategic planning can be a relatively quick and straightforward review of mission, vision, values, and current programs, or it can include extensive research and analysis and cost hundreds of thousands of dollars. While it's up to boards and chief executives to determine what process is right for their organizations, the distinction between strategic planning and business planning is worth discussion because board members often confuse the two or use the terms interchangeably.

Strategic planning is a process organizations use to review their fundamental purpose and plan their future direction, typically for the next three to five years. It may also include a financial plan for implementation, but a majority of strategic plans do not.

Business planning is usually done in the context of a specific product, program, or service, and business plans usually include an examination of the market or need, a competitive analysis, information about the project team, and financial analysis and projections. Business plans rarely look more than three years into the future. Business planning is sometimes used for startup organizations or for an entire organization when it only offers one service or does one thing.

Whatever form planning takes and whatever the final product is called, chief executives and boards need to recognize that implementing a plan often requires additional financial and human resources, and failure to consider the resources needed for implementation increases the likelihood that the plan will end up gathering dust.

Key Questions

- When was the last time our organization reviewed the context for our work, engaged current stakeholders, and thought about the future of the organization?

- What are the two or three key challenges we need to address or decisions we need to make in order for the board and chief executive to have a clear shared vision for the future? Who else should have a voice in those decisions, and how could they be engaged in the process?

- If we currently have a strategic plan, are we following it and making progress? What human and financial resources do we need to successfully implement our current plan? Do we have a realistic plan for getting them?

CHAPTER 7
Develop Future Leadership

Because the future of any organization depends on its ability to attract new board and staff leaders, one of the chief executive's primary and most often neglected responsibilities is to develop future leaders within the board and staff.

Within the staff, this responsibility is relatively uncomplicated. The chief executive should hire staff members who have the potential for an increased leadership role and provide opportunities for them to develop those skills. This may translate into actions such as offering competitive salaries that will attract highly qualified applicants, protecting professional development budgets even in times of financial stress, and learning to delegate so that others can develop their leadership skills and their sense of responsibility.

The chief executive's role in developing future board leadership is equally critical but less prominent. Chief executives should be, by virtue of their position, members of the governance or nominating committee — not simply to take notes and provide logistical support, but as active participants. Some executives may shy away from this role, while others wish they could handpick officers and new board members or at least have absolute veto power. Neither of these extremes is good for the long-term health of the organization or for a healthy balance of power between executive and board.

Chief executives should play an active role in developing board leadership for several reasons. As they interact with other community leaders, volunteers, clients and patrons, parents, and other constituents, they are well positioned to spot talent and commitment to the organization. In addition, the success of the board chair and other board leaders depends on their ability to forge a successful partnership with the chief executive. While chief executives should build positive professional relationships with anyone the board selects for a leadership role, the executive's insights and opinions should carry considerable weight in the selection process.

When the executive dominates the selection of board members and officers, some of the organization's vitality is sacrificed along with a measure of the board's independence and authority. Board members who have contacts outside the executive's sphere of influence can recruit board members with new skills and networks who can, in turn, expand the organization's contacts even further. In contrast, manipulative executives can consolidate their own power and encourage board complacency by suggesting weak officers and lackluster board candidates or candidates with whom they have close personal ties. Active participation from the chief executive in developing board leadership is a good thing. Domination is not.

Many chief executives think about the possibility of their own departure, but few take steps to increase the likelihood of a thoughtful and orderly transition. Most wouldn't know where to start, for a variety of reasons. Many nonprofit chief executives — particularly those who founded an organization or have served for a long time — have a strong affinity for the mission and a sense of identity that is intertwined with the organization. They think about their departure only with reluctance.

Further, most executives want to leave on their own timetable and hesitate to do anything that might result in their departure ahead of schedule. Many nonprofits, particularly smaller community-based organizations, don't have the resources to hire a deputy director or a senior management team that could furnish an internal successor to the current executive. And situations in which there could be a strong internal candidate create additional complications since grooming a successor without interfering with the board's prerogative to choose the new leader can be tricky.

Here are two steps that all chief executives can take to reduce the organization's dependence on a single leader:

1. *Write things down.* Chief executives should consider the possibility that they might leave their position unexpectedly and imagine what a successor's first few days and weeks on the job might be like. Are policies and procedures collected somewhere in writing? Are position descriptions up to date? This may seem obvious, or tactical rather than strategic, but

a surprising number of new executives waste precious weeks or months sorting out byzantine procedures and unwritten policies. After taking the time to document, collect, and update this information, many chief executives may find themselves more effective in their current role, even if they aren't planning on leaving any time soon.

2. *Create a transition plan.* This does *not* mean identifying a successor or committing to a timetable. It might mean suggesting someone on staff who would be capable of serving as an interim chief executive, discussing how the board would approach an executive search if one were needed, assembling a list of potential search consultants and updating it periodically, or making sure that board officers have access to information they'd need to make decisions in the event of an unexpected transition. Because this suggestion is akin to planning one's own funeral, it will always require sensitivity on the part of board and executive.

A final element of the executive's responsibility for building future leadership is to make the chief executive job look doable. Working around the clock, keeping the chief executive's salary artificially low, or soldiering on without adequate administrative support may feel heroic and necessary. But such practices, which are prevalent throughout the nonprofit sector, make it more difficult for boards to hire successors when current executives retire and reduce the likelihood that younger staff members will aspire to be chief executives.

Many studies have predicted a nonprofit sector "leadership deficit" as large numbers of current chief executives leave their jobs or retire. While it's true that many current executives are reaching retirement age, there's no evidence that younger people don't want to step into these roles. In fact, there's plenty of evidence that they do.

Large numbers of young people want to work in the nonprofit sector, and many aspire to be chief executives. Studies have shown that younger people do have some reservations about the chief executive role. They are concerned about work-life balance, being responsible for fundraising, and the consequences of failure. However, current chief executives should not be concerned that a new generation of leaders won't step up to the plate.

Key Questions

- Have we identified and cultivated likely successors to the current board chair and other key leadership posts?

- If the chief executive were to depart unexpectedly, does the board know what its immediate next steps would be, and are there systems in place to ensure that the organization's work can continue smoothly while the organization transitions to new leadership?

- What are we doing as an organization to support and develop staff members who can take on increased leadership roles in the future?

CHAPTER 8

Build External Relationships and Serve as an Advocate

More than any other individual leader, the chief executive serves as the public face of a nonprofit organization. Board leaders and other senior staff members can and should represent the organization to the public and help build relationships with other individuals and organizations — including funders, partners, and policymakers. However, the chief executive does this most visibly and consistently. For that reason, chief executives need to have strong interpersonal and communications skills. Those who don't must find the support and resources needed to develop their abilities over time.

The critical skills and tools every chief executive should have include

- A concise and compelling "elevator speech" that explains the organization and its work. Board members and other staff also need this speech, and executives often use media or communications consultants to help board and staff members fine-tune and practice these messages.

- An understanding of the laws that govern nonprofit lobbying activities. Although nonprofits are free to lobby, there are limits on the percentage of an organization's budget that can be spent on direct lobbying. Nonprofits are prohibited from participating in political campaigns by supporting a candidate.

- Diplomacy, tact, and political skills. Although it may seem self-evident, a chief executive who lacks these skills may face challenges in working with the board and with other external partners. Single-mindedness and strong advocacy for the executive's own organization need to be balanced with consideration for the needs and positions of others.

- The ability to follow through on commitments. Chief executives are often stretched thin professionally. To be successful at building external partnerships, executives need to make sure they (and their organization) have the bandwidth to follow through on the promises they make — or risk developing a reputation as an unreliable partner. Good intentions are not enough.

- An organizational structure and resources to support their external leadership. This includes a Web site and other communications vehicles that deliver key messages and communications staff or consultants who can assist with media relations, testimony preparation, and other specialized activities. The organization's board should also be structured to support external leadership. Communications and policy expertise should be among the skill sets represented on the board. Depending on the organization's needs, the board may also want to form a public policy committee to provide guidance on policy and advocacy work. (Communications committees, on the other hand, often end up micromanaging or duplicating work being done by staff members and are most appropriate for small organizations where board members are actually doing hands-on communications work.)

Chief executives who are preoccupied with internal management challenges may find it difficult to embrace or find time for their external role as an advocate, communicator, and relationship builder. Executives who struggle with this dilemma should recognize that internal matters can often be delegated much more easily than external leadership. If the chief executive fails to engage with policymakers, identify opportunities to collaborate with other organizations, or seek out community leadership roles, the work will usually go undone and the organization's visibility or reputation may suffer.

The chief executive should be the primary spokesperson and representative of the organization, particularly in smaller nonprofits. However, giving other staff and board leaders the skills and authority to represent the organization is an important part of developing their leadership skills, and chief executives should look for such opportunities.

In creating a successful partnership, the board and the chief executive should be clear about who speaks on behalf of the organization and who is ultimately responsible for building relationships. In both cases, the answer is usually the chief executive. Board members may be called on to make introductions, testify at a public hearing, accompany the executive to a critical meeting, and support advocacy in other ways. Similarly, the chief executive should establish clear internal guidelines for staff members about what they are authorized to do and in what circumstances.

The board has a policy role in supporting the chief executive and protecting the interests of the organization. The board may want to establish some boundaries to guide the chief executive in building external relationships and serving as a public spokesperson. Examples might include establishing a process for taking a position on a legislative or public policy issue, developing clear guidelines about who is authorized to speak on behalf of the organization and in what circumstances, and embedding the expectation for external leadership into the chief executive's annual performance goals.

Key Questions

- Are we clear on who is authorized to speak on behalf of the organization, and have those people received training and developed the skills to do so effectively?

- Does the chief executive's current job description and range of responsibilities allow enough time for external leadership? Have the chief executive and the board identified external leadership as a priority?

- Does our organization have the resources, staff, and tools needed to support the chief executive's external leadership roles? If not, can we reallocate resources, or raise additional funds?

CHAPTER 9
Ensure the Quality and Effectiveness of Programs

Monitoring the quality and effectiveness of individual programs and the organization as a whole is almost entirely the responsibility of the chief executive, often with assistance from staff and external consultants or advisors. Without the chief executive's cooperation and support, most boards will not have enough data or programmatic expertise to have a sensible discussion about program evaluation, impact, or outcomes.

The chief executive's role in ensuring quality and effectiveness cuts across many of the responsibilities discussed earlier and includes

- listening to the community, clients or program participants, public officials, and grantmakers to better understand what the organization is expected to accomplish

- developing a logic model or theory of change[4] that explains what the organization is trying to accomplish, describes why and how, and proposes ways to measure effectiveness

- allocating sufficient financial, human, and technology resources to collect information about the people being served, track changes and impact over time, and measure success

---

4 Logic models, theories of change, and outcome-based evaluation are systems of thinking that have evolved to help nonprofits think more clearly about strategy and impact. Each involves a significant literature and a distinct vocabulary, but the underlying principles are similar.

- using the information captured through evaluation and assessment to make management decisions and strengthen programs

- helping the board of directors frame periodic discussions about program effectiveness, particularly when programs are added or discontinued or when more resources are needed to improve quality or expand

A surprising number of nonprofits fail to collect basic data or answer the most obvious questions about their work — how many people they serve, income and geographic breakdown of clients or patrons, how demand or participation has changed over time, or client success rates. The inability of some organizations to answer these questions is understandable. Many nonprofits are short-staffed, lack adequate technology, or are focused on meeting immediate and urgent client needs. Over the long haul, however, such organizations stand a poor chance of improving their performance or making a compelling case for why they should be supported. An effective chief executive will support evaluation as an opportunity for organizational learning and continuous improvement and will make sure that board and staff members are asking the right questions. Examples of questions to ask around evaluation include the following:

- Do we have enough information to make the case that our work is needed?

- Are we clear about what we're trying to accomplish? What evidence do we have that our programs are effective or that our approach works?

- What's our definition of success? Can it be measured or documented, and are we currently making any effort to do so?

- Do we understand the difference between activities and outcomes, and do we take the time to evaluate both?

- Do we have solid data on the people we serve and what we do for them?

- Do we understand the true cost of providing our programs? Is the cost justified given the outcomes we produce? If we had more resources, could we produce better results?

KEY QUESTIONS

- Do we know enough about our work to make a strong case about why we're effective and worthy of donor support?

- Is our primary interest in evaluation to satisfy the needs of third parties, such as sources of funding, or do we want better information so that we can improve our program, change our approach, or tell our story more effectively?

- How much money are we willing to spend on evaluation, and how will we use what we learn?

CHAPTER 10
Support the Board

The preceding nine responsibilities present the nonprofit executive with a long list of tasks and admonitions — any three or four combined are enough to create a challenging full-time job. In addition to everything else, the executive is responsible for supporting the board. Depending on the executive's temperament and the nature of the existing partnership, chief executives' attitudes about this responsibility range from denial to grudging acceptance to enthusiastic embrace.

Yes, boards are responsible for "organizing themselves to be effective." However, as in so many of the executive responsibilities discussed here, the board can't do its job without information, direction, administrative support, and encouragement from the chief executive. Carefully crafted meeting agendas, committee structures that are aligned with the needs of the organization, and thoughtful and strategic discussions will not spring into existence out of the raw material supplied by the board members, no matter how much energy and good will they bring to the table. The chief executive is the catalyst whose active participation is needed to take board performance from bad to good and from good to great.

In their insightful book, *Executive Leadership in Nonprofit Organizations,* researchers Robert Herman and Richard Heimovics noted that the most effective chief executives have discovered that they can get more done for the organization by embracing their responsibility for helping the board do its job. Herman and Heimovics described these effective executives as "board-centered." The set of behaviors described below are adapted loosely from their work.

Chief executives who embrace their responsibility for supporting the board do the following:

- *Initiate and maintain a structure for board work.* In most organizations, the chief executive (sometimes through another staff member but sometimes directly) sends out meeting notices, coordinates meeting times and locations, orders food, sends out the agenda and other advance materials, and makes sure that accurate minutes are taken and eventually distributed. The chief executive may do the same for some or all board committees. These superficial duties are not worth much further discussion except to reaffirm that they are almost universally accepted and practiced as executive responsibilities. Performed poorly, they can have a surprisingly large impact on overall board performance. The board-centered chief executive makes these responsibilities a priority and does them well.

- *Work in close partnership with the board chair to plan efficient and productive meetings.* This goes beyond simply putting together an agenda and may include a pre-meeting session with the chair to discuss goals and desired outcomes for the meeting; creating a timed and annotated agenda to help the board chair run the meeting well; designing, administering, and tabulating results from a meeting evaluation form; and having a post-meeting session to review decisions and next steps. An overcommitted board chair may not have enough time for all these steps, in which case the chief executive needs to find less time-consuming ways to accomplish the same things. Many chief executives also work with the chair to create an annual calendar to guide the board's work.

- *Show consideration and respect to board members and facilitate interaction in board relationships.* No matter how committed, the board chair is not likely to be able to develop a one-on-one relationship with every board member. The board-centered chief executive will make this a priority and will work to ensure that all board members feel equally valued and participate fully in the work of the board. This includes taking the time to understand the positions, concerns, and interests of individual board members, which reduces the likelihood that the chief executive will be surprised or sidelined during board discussions. It also includes understanding what each board member finds rewarding or valuable in serving on the board and responding to those needs.

- *Provide helpful and useful information to the board.* The chief executive needs to work with the board chair and other officers to make sure that the board receives the right information — and the right quantity of information — at the right time to support its work. While a few executives provide too little information, many others provide too much. Successful chief executives manage to find a balance, which will vary from organization to organization and is also likely to change over time. The chief executive's goal should be to make board members feel smart, not to stupefy them with overwhelming amounts of unedited material. One of the most valuable ways chief executives can spend their time is editing, simplifying, and clarifying information that is given to the board.

- *Promote board accomplishments and productivity.* One of the characteristics of an effective team is a culture of mutual accountability.[5] While chief executives are not well positioned to point out the shortcomings of the board as a whole or of individual directors, they can do so indirectly by making sure that performance is recognized and acknowledged. If board members or board committees who do their jobs and produce results receive no more recognition than those who consistently fall short, the performance of the entire board is likely, over time, to fall to the lowest acceptable level of productivity. Board members are more likely to follow through on their commitments if they consistently see examples of other board members who do so. And the board as a whole is more likely to produce meaningful results if it is reminded of past successes and convinced that its work is vital to the organization.

5   See *The Wisdom of Teams* by Jon R. Katzenbach and Douglas K.Smith, 2003. This book falls outside the usual realm of nonprofit management and leadership literature, but is extremely useful for examining the partnership between the board and chief executive as a team.

- *Envision change and innovation with the board.* An effective chief executive keeps the board informed about trends and changes in the external environment and their implications for the organization and the work of the board. In addition to the formal planning process, discussed earlier, the executive should play this role on an ongoing basis. Executives should lay the groundwork for change over time so that major shifts or decision points don't come as a surprise to the board. This applies both to the work of the organization and that of the board itself. Effective chief executives are not content with business as usual and use their position to encourage ongoing adaptation and improvement.

Recommending that the chief executive take responsibility for the success of the board is not equivalent to suggesting that the chief executive manipulate or dominate the board. Executives who do can sometimes be successful over the short term or even for many years. But the opportunity cost is huge. Chief executives who dominate their organizations' boards not only fail to capitalize on a potential asset but also create a climate of reduced accountability and increased risk. As a result, the executive's leadership role is lonelier and more precarious than it would otherwise need to be.

The chief executive's role in supporting the board extends, sometimes awkwardly, to supporting the board in conducting the executive's annual performance assessment and salary review. Thus, many chief executives find themselves helping the board identify an assessment tool, gathering comparable salary information, and reminding the board chair that the review needs to take place. Even chief executives who understand their responsibility for the board's success may still feel sheepish reminding the board chair that they haven't had a performance review in two years or suggesting that a long-overdue raise be made retroactive.

Working with the board chair to create an annual work plan for the board and making sure the performance and salary review are part of that plan will drain some of the awkwardness from the interaction. In addition, any chief executive who has witnessed the occasional distortions in the space-time continuum that occur at board meetings — a board member suggests something that was discussed and adopted at the previous meeting or the chair talks about a policy approved two years ago as if it were still under discussion — should not feel self-conscious about reminding the board that the chief executive assessment is overdue.

The chief executive may also need to help the board initiate a periodic assessment of its own effectiveness since many boards find the idea of self-assessment threatening or off-putting. Chief executives who fully embrace the behaviors described in the bullets above will recognize the importance of board self-assessment as a tool for improving the systems and structures that support board work, increasing board productivity, and stimulating innovation and change. The executive may need to help the board find a consultant or a self-assessment tool, develop a plan for conducting the self-assessment, provide some administrative support, and offer reassurance that the process can be positive and productive.

When considering their role in supporting the board, chief executives should review the concept of servant-leadership, which was mentioned briefly in the introduction. If the board and executive focus on their roles in serving and supporting each other, rather than traditional hierarchical ideas about who's in charge, a balanced partnership is more likely to emerge. The chief executive will sometimes lead the board but will often create the space and provide the tools for the board to lead.

This long list of suggestions may cause some chief executives to wonder whether they have time to do all these things, given everything else they have to do, and wonder what percentage of their time they should be willing to dedicate to supporting and working with the board.

The national survey that led to *Daring to Lead 2011* asked more than 3,000 chief executives how much time they spent on their boards. A majority of respondents said they spent 10 hours or fewer per month working with their boards — which translates to just 6 percent of their time. Respondents who reported spending very little time with their boards also reported significantly lower levels of satisfaction with their board's performance than executives who spent more time. Many highly effective chief executives interviewed for *Daring to Lead* and other studies reported spending much more of their time on their boards — many saying they spent 20 to 25 percent of their time on board-related matters.

While that level of investment may seem high for leaders who are pulled in many directions, the most effective executives recognize that their own success — and the organization's — depends on the board's effectiveness. Those who embrace their own responsibility for the board's success, rather than passively complaining about a weak board, are more likely to succeed themselves.

KEY QUESTIONS

- Does the chief executive spend enough time supporting the board? If not, what responsibilities could be delegated or shifted so that the executive could focus more time and attention on helping the board be effective?

- Has the board recently completed a self-assessment of its own performance, and have any changes been made as a result?

- Could questions about the chief executive's partnership with the board be incorporated into a future self-assessment, or into the chief executive's annual performance review?

CONCLUSION

This publication began with a discussion of the challenges inherent in the chief executive's role — challenges that are widely recognized and increasingly well documented. But focusing exclusively on the ambiguities and frustrations facing chief executives would be misleading.

Many chief executives speak eloquently about the rewards of their jobs and the pride they take in their work. Leading a nonprofit organization involves an enormous variety of tasks and responsibilities that change over time. Chief executives are almost never bored. They have an unusual amount of professional autonomy that includes opportunities for creativity and ongoing personal and professional development. They often put in long hours but do so knowing that they are working hard for a cause in which they believe.

Nonprofit chief executives receive recognition and visibility within their communities and often build lasting relationships with board members and colleagues who share their interests and values. Many successful long-term leaders can look back at their careers with pride and satisfaction, knowing that they have helped build extraordinary institutions that are improving lives and communities. Few careers offer such a compelling combination of benefits.

Robert Herman and Richard Heimovics, writing in the early 1990s after extensive studies of leadership and management in nonprofit organizations, suggested that the most effective nonprofit executives have "discovered that it is their special kind of leadership that is essential to the accomplishment of the critically important goals of the nonprofit sector in our society."

A growing number of board members, grantmakers, and other nonprofit sector stakeholders have reached the same conclusion. The chief executive is pivotal and essential, and the future of the nonprofit sector depends on the ability of nonprofits to attract and retain talented and visionary chief executives who have a clear understanding of their role and perform it well.

APPENDIX I

NONPROFIT CHIEF EXECUTIVE JOB DESCRIPTION

The chief executive works in partnership with the board of directors and the staff to provide leadership, vision, and direction for the organization and to develop an organizational strategy. The chief executive implements policies approved by the board, manages the organization's programs and operations, and represents the organization in the community. Specific responsibilities include

- overseeing the development, implementation, and evaluation of programs and services that support the mission

- leading the staff and board in developing a realistic annual budget and making financial decisions consistent with the budget as approved by the board

- developing a staffing structure that supports the efficient delivery of programs and services, accomplishment of major goals identified in the strategic plan, and effective overall management

- hiring and managing the staff, including the implementation and ongoing revision of personnel policies approved by the board and managing the staff performance review process

- leading fundraising efforts, including supporting the board's involvement in fundraising, personally cultivating and soliciting donors, and supervising development staff and implementation of fundraising plans and policies approved by the board

- providing regular, timely internal financial statements to the board of directors that compare performance to budget and to the previous year or other benchmark

- planning for adequate cash flow to cover operational needs

- conducting multiyear financial analysis, analyzing trends, and engaging the board in strategic discussions about financial stability and sustainability, including the development of adequate operating reserves

- complying with all local, state, and federal legal requirements

- building positive relationships with partner organizations, policymakers, media, and others

- representing the organization by participating in key associations and organizations, serving on committees and advisory groups, and speaking in public settings

APPENDIX II

PERSONAL QUALITIES OF EFFECTIVE CHIEF EXECUTIVES

Serving as the chief executive of a nonprofit organization requires a wide variety of skills and attributes. Some, such as the ability to be a team player, juggle multiple tasks and responsibilities simultaneously, or communicate well, would appear on the list of desired characteristics for almost any senior management position. Those listed below are more specific to the role of the nonprofit chief executive.

1. **Integrity.** The board, the staff, and the community need to perceive the executive as honest, trustworthy, and operating in the best interests of the organization and the larger community or cause.

2. **Credibility.** Chief executives can achieve credibility through professional credentials and accomplishments; a close personal connection to an organization, cause, or community; or a track record of promises kept and results delivered over time.

3. **Charisma.** Beyond being a skilled communicator, the chief executive should be a compelling presence — able to speak about the work of the organization in powerful and inspiring terms, able to command attention and inspire confidence, and able to motivate others to follow and give.

4. **Initiative.** Chief executives can build the capacity for initiative at many levels of the organization but are unlikely to be successful if they don't possess a considerable degree of personal courage, resourcefulness, and ingenuity. The most effective chief executives have the confidence to act, rather than always waiting passively for direction from others.

5. **Vision.** Successful chief executives are aware of the gap between current reality and what should be. Whether the vision involves increased success and impact for the organization, expanded services for the community, or significant social change, the chief executive can see a better future and has faith that it can become a reality.

6. **Competence.** Charisma and vision complement but do not replace actual skill. Chief executives need content and program expertise, as well as financial and general management skills. The board and other staff members can compensate for some weak areas, but not for overall incompetence.

7. **Responsiveness.** Effective chief executives listen well — to the community, staff, board members, stakeholders, and partners — and respond appropriately.

APPENDIX III

TEN QUESTIONS FOR NONPROFIT CHIEF EXECUTIVES

Many self-assessments ask chief executives to consider their performance or understanding of their responsibilities in very broad or abstract terms. The following questions are designed to bridge the gap between theory and reality by addressing actual situations and concrete actions. Chief executives who are honest in their responses can use this brief self-assessment to identify areas where improvement is needed.

1. Does your organization's mission statement accurately reflect its current work and priorities?

   a. Yes

   b. No

   c. I can't call it to mind.

2. The last time you attended a social event and someone asked about your profession, how did you respond?

   a. Gave a short yet compelling commercial for my organization and its work

   b. Tried to change the subject

   c. Mumbled something about running a nonprofit

3. Think back to the most recent employee who resigned. What is your internal response?

   a. Confidence that qualified and capable candidates would find the organization and the position appealing

   b. Relief

   c. Anxiety because I didn't think I could find a replacement who would work for the pittance we were paying

4. How much operating cash does your organization currently have in the bank?

   a. More than 90 days

   b. Fewer than 30 days

   c. No idea

4. Is your level of unrestricted net assets higher or lower than it was three years ago?

   a. Higher

   b. Lower

   c. No idea

6. Do you know who your next board chair is likely to be?

   a. Yes

   b. No

   c. Are you kidding?

7. Consider the last three people elected to the board. How were the majority suggested?

   a. By me

   b. By other board members

   c. By picking names at random from the phone book

   d. We haven't elected three new people while I've been chief executive.

8. Who approves your expense reports and requests for reimbursement?

   a. The board chair

   b. I do.

   c. Someone who reports to me

9. If you were to leave your position today, would anyone on the staff be a credible candidate for your position?

   a. Yes

   b. No

   c. Why are you asking? I'm not planning on going anywhere.

10. At the last board meeting, who talked the most?

    a. Difficult to say

    b. I did.

    c. The board chair

Key: This tool is intended to break the ice and start conversations, and wasn't really designed to be scored. Nonetheless, the preferred answers are:

1. a. Of course. If you answered b, you may be overdue for strategic planning, and if you answered c, you may be in the wrong job.

2. a. Almost everyone in the nonprofit sector has experienced awkwardness or difficulty explaining to others what we do. This question points to the importance of having a compelling "elevator" speech — and taking justifiable pride in your role as a nonprofit chief executive.

3. a. If you answered b, you may have let a challenging situation go on for too long without taking action for the good of the organization. (It's still okay to be relieved, though.) If you answered c, low salaries and poor benefits may be undermining your organization's ability to attract talent and fulfill its mission.

4. a. Obviously, you have to tell the truth. Most experts suggest a minimum of three months' of reserves. And if you don't know, you should.

5. a or b. Again, a would be better than c. Either way, you should be able to answer this question off the top of your head.

6. a. Succession planning for board leaders is just as important — perhaps even more important — than for paid staff, since most board leaders serve for a defined term. A strong board will be full of potential leaders, and should have a process for creating a pipeline.

7. a or b. Most people will answer either a or b. Ideally, the board should be identifying a majority of candidates, but most chief executives play a central role.

8. a. Probably. Whoever approves your expense reports should be someone with enough authority to ask questions and not sign off automatically. An employee who works for you may not be the best choice.

9. a. Maybe. Chief executives are under no obligation to line up an internal successor. For small organizations, this may not be possible, and in all organizations the responsibility for choosing a new executive lies with the board. Whether the answer is a or b, raising the issue should not prompt defensiveness on the part of the executive.

10. a. The most effective boards find a way to engage many board members in board discussions. While meetings dominated by the board chair or by the executive are common, neither is desirable.

SUGGESTED RESOURCES

Axelrod, Nancy R. *Chief Executive Succession Planning: Essential Guidance for Boards and CEOs, Second Edition.* Washington, DC: BoardSource, 2010.

Chief executive succession planning is not only about determining your organization's next leader. It is a continuous process that assesses your organization's needs and identifies leadership that supports those needs. A successful succession plan is linked to the strategic plan, mission, and vision. Author Nancy Axelrod helps board members prepare for the future by examining the ongoing and intermittent steps of executive succession planning.

BoardSource. *The Source: Twelve Principles of Governance That Power Exceptional Boards.* Washington, DC: BoardSource, 2005.

Exceptional boards add significant value to their organizations, making discernible differences in their advance on mission. *The Source* defines governance not as dry, obligatory compliance but as a creative and collaborative process that supports chief executives, engages board members, and furthers the causes they all serve. Aspirational in nature, these principles offer chief executives a description of an empowered board that is a strategic asset to be leveraged; they provide board members with a vision of what is possible and a way to add lasting value to the organizations they lead.

Chait, Richard P., William P. Ryan, and Barbara E. Taylor. *Governance as Leadership: Reframing the Work of Nonprofit Boards.* Hoboken, NJ: John Wiley & Sons, Inc., 2005.

Written about the board rather than the chief executive, this book still speaks eloquently about the changing role of nonprofit chief executives — acknowledging that they have become de facto leaders and providing advice about how leadership can be shared between board and executive to tap the full potential of the board.

Cornelius, Marla, Rick Moyers, and Jeanne Bell. *Daring to Lead 2011: A National Study of Executive Director Leadership.* San Francisco: CompassPoint Nonprofit Services and the Meyer Foundation, 2011.

CompassPoint and the Meyer Foundation have conducted three national studies of nonprofit executives since 2001. The most recent was based on responses from more than 3,000 nonprofit chief executives in 11 cities across the United States; it reported on projected rates of executive transition and the impact of the Great Recession on executives and their organizations. The full report, companion briefs, and reports from 2006 and 2001 can be downloaded at www.daringtolead.org.

Dambach, Charles F., Melissa Davis, and Robert L. Gale. *Structures and Practices of Nonprofit Boards, Second Edition.* Washington, DC: BoardSource, 2009.

Strong nonprofit board leadership is important to the success of your organization. This book clarifies the difference in the roles of the chief executive and board chair and provides suggestions for how this partnership can be strengthened. Discover how this leadership can effectively work with the governance committee to facilitate board development. Don't miss the sample job descriptions.

Grace, Kay Sprinkel, Amy McClellan, and John A. Yankey. *The Nonprofit Board's Role in Mission, Planning, and Evaluation, Second Edition.* Washington, DC: BoardSource, 2009.

Is your board actively supporting and advancing your organization's mission? Learn how board members can actively contribute to the creation of mission as well as communicate the mission and purpose to the community. Discover how your board can partner with organizational staff to implement mission and supporting policies.

Greenleaf, Robert K. *Servant Leadership: A Journey into the Nature of Legitimate Power and Greatness.* Mawhah, NJ: Paulist Press, 2002.

Many of the author's best known essays on servant-leadership, including "The Servant as Leader," "The Institution as Servant," and "Trustees as Servants," are collected in this one volume. Greenleaf's notion that people must be servants first and leaders second continues to influence the broader field of leadership development, and provides a useful context for thinking about the relationship between the board and the chief executive.

Herman, Robert D. and Richard D. Heimovics. *Executive Leadership in Nonprofit Organizations: New Strategies for Shaping Board-Staff Dynamics.* San Francisco: Jossey-Bass, 1991.

This seminal book makes a compelling distinction between chief executives who view themselves as the passive victims of ineffective boards and those who take responsibility for the board's success, and argues persuasively for the latter. This book is not as well known as it should be, and is worth revisiting every few years for fresh insight.

Ingram, Richard T. *Ten Basic Responsibilities of Nonprofit Boards, Second Edition.* Washington, DC: BoardSource, 2009.

One of the most widely distributed and best known nonprofit management and leadership publications, Ingram's book outlines basic board responsibilities and complements *The Nonprofit Chief Executive's Ten Basic Responsiblities.*

Mintz, Joshua and Jane Pierson. *Assessment of the Chief Executive.* Washington, DC: BoardSource, 2005.

This flexible and practical tool is designed to assist boards in their annual responsibility for assessing the performance of the chief executive. After discussing the benefits of assessment, the user's guide suggests a process and provides a questionnaire that addresses every major area of responsibility. Also included is a self-evaluation form for the executive to complete and share with the board. This resource is also available in a quick and easy-to-use online version. Contact BoardSource for more details.

Robinson, Maureen K. *Nonprofit Boards that Work: The End of One-Size-Fits-All Governance.* Hoboken, NJ: John Wiley & Sons, Inc., 2000.

This thoughtful and pragmatic examination of the board's role includes a short chapter on the working partnership between the executive and the board, but is permeated with good advice for nonprofit executives.

Waechter, Susan A. *Driving Strategic Planning: A Nonprofit Executive's Guide.* Washington, DC: BoardSource, 2010.

This book will help you learn how to work with your staff and board to assess the readiness of your organization and prepare for strategic planning. Discover a variety of approaches for dealing with common issues and overcoming organizational resistance to beginning the process. Review the fundamental elements of the strategic planning process, from mission and vision to environmental scan and competitive analysis.

Williams, Sherrill K. and Kathleen A. McGinnis. *Building the Governance Partnership: The Chief Executive's Guide to Getting the Best from the Board.* Washington, DC: BoardSource, 2011.

This book offers practical tips and perspectives to help chief executives build a partnership with the board that is based on support, trust, honesty, forthrightness, respect, and understanding. Chief executives will learn how to establish the board culture that is right for their organization, practice self-management and cultivate relationships, inform and communicate with the board, facilitate a balance in roles and responsibilities, structure the board's work, and plan for transitions. Each chapter ends with short essays written by a chief executive and a board chair, providing unique perspectives and a personal touch to the topics covered.

Wilson, Judith and Michelle Gislason. *Coaching Skills for Nonprofit Managers and Leaders: Developing People to Achieve Your Mission.* San Francisco: Jossey-Bass, 2009.

This book provides nonprofit managers with an understanding of why and how to coach, how to initiate coaching in specific situations, how to make coaching really work, and how to refine coaching for long-term success. It offers practical steps for coaching leaders to greatness and can be used as a thorough topical overview or as a quick reference or refresher. This book uses accessible language, examples, case studies, key questions, and exercises.

The Annie E. Casey Foundation has produced several excellent publications that explore the issues surrounding executive transition. They can be downloaded from the foundation's Web site at www.aecf.org.

ABOUT THE AUTHOR

Rick Moyers is vice president for programs and communications at the Eugene and Agnes E. Meyer Foundation in Washington, D.C. Rick has led the Meyer Foundation's nationally recognized capacity-building work since joining the foundation as program officer for its Nonprofit Sector Fund in 2003. From 1999 to 2003, Rick was executive director of the Ohio Association of Nonprofit Organizations, and from 1992 to 1999 he held senior management positions at BoardSource.

A frequent speaker on nonprofit management and leadership issues, Rick is a co-author of the *Daring to Lead 2006* and *Daring to Lead 2011* national studies of nonprofit executive directors, produced in collaboration with CompassPoint, and the author of "Against the Grain," a popular *Chronicle of Philanthropy* blog about nonprofit boards.

In 2009, Rick was the co-recipient of the Alliance for Nonprofit Management's inaugural Grantmaker in Capacity Building Award, which recognized both his and the Meyer Foundation's longstanding commitment to building the field of nonprofit management and leadership. He currently serves on the boards of the Washington Regional Association of Grantmakers and the Community Connections Fund of the World Bank, and is a past board member of Imagination Stage, a family theater in Bethesda, Md.

Rick is a graduate of Washington Adventist University in Takoma Park, Md., and holds a master's degree from the University of Baltimore. He is also an instructor for The Grantmaking School, a program of the Johnson Center for Philanthropy at Grand Valley State University in Michigan.

AUTHOR'S NOTE

For more than 20 years, I've worked in organizations that sought to strengthen the management and leadership of nonprofits. Over that time, I've talked with hundreds of nonprofit executives about their partnership with the board and the broader management aspects of their jobs.

Serving as executive director of the Ohio Association of Nonprofit Organizations from 1999 to 2003 was in many ways the most challenging, consuming, and rewarding thing I've ever done. I wish I could say that I always followed the advice in this book when I was a chief executive. Sometimes I did, but some of my insights also come from my own missteps.

I'd like to acknowledge the many ways in which friends and colleagues contributed to this publication. In particular, the many outstanding chief executives I've met over the years — too many to list — give me confidence that the job can be done with grace, skill, and style. Those chief executives are my heroes.